Listening Effectively

John A. Kline

Air University Press
Maxwell Air Force Base, Alabama

April 1996

Library of Congress Cataloging-in-Publication Data

Kline, John A.
    Listening effectively / John A. Kline.
      p.   cm.
    1. Listening.   I. Title.
    BF323.L5K55   1996   95-552799
    153.6'8—dc20   CIP

ISBN 1-58566-009-4

First Printing April 1996
Second Printing July 2000
Third Printing August 2001

Disclaimer

For Sale by the Superintendent of Documents
US Government Printing Office
Washington, DC 20402

Contents

Illustrations

Foreword

Though it's perhaps the most important of our communication skills, listening is one of the most neglected. Our lack of attention to listening skills is puzzling; we spend so much of our time listening that its importance cannot be challenged. Yet the obvious explanation is that most of us believe we listen well.

In *Listening Effectively*, Dr Kline describes the importance of good listening in a variety of settings, from life-and-death situations to the sort of everyday situations in which you and I find ourselves all too often. He then explains how we can become the good listeners we all want to be. But, he points out, learning to listen well requires considerable effort on our part. The good news is that the rewards for enhancing our listening skills are more than worth the effort.

Dr Kline addresses this intriguing topic in straightforward, understandable terms. The result is a very readable and helpful book—concise, yet comprehensive; entertaining, yet informative; lively, yet serious. As a companion volume to his outstanding *Speaking Effectively: A Guide to Air Force Speakers*, I heartily recommend *Listening Effectively*.

BILLY J. BOLES
General, USAF
Commander, Air Education and
Training Command

About the
Author

Dr John A. Kline

Dr John A. Kline is a senior executive (SES) and Academic Provost for Air University. He received his BS from Iowa State University. He held an NDEA Fellowship while earning MS and PhD degrees at the University of Iowa.

Dr Kline was professor of communication at the universities of New Mexico and Missouri–Columbia. He has been at Air University since 1975 as professor, dean, educational advisor, and finally as provost.

Dr Kline has written books, presented many papers, and published widely in leading professional journals. He is an accomplished speaker, he has lectured extensively throughout the Air Force, and he has presented many speeches to a variety of military, professional, religious, and corporate organizations worldwide.

Listening Effectively is a companion volume to his widely read *Speaking Effectively.*

Preface

Listening Effectively takes a "how to" approach to the listening process. Everyone can be a better listener. This book provides information to help in a logical and practical way.

To lay the groundwork for the rest of the book, the first chapter presents the need for better listening. This discussion covers, among other things, the fact that few people have ever received any formal training in effective listening. Some real-life examples of the need for better listening are given.

The second chapter focuses on things we think are true about listening, but are not; that is, common fallacies about listening. Those who know these fallacies can probably use a refresher. And those who haven't been exposed to them before should benefit greatly, though some may find it difficult to release erroneous beliefs.

The third chapter discusses the listening process, from receiving sound waves to taking action on remembered instructions. Five steps of the process are explained: receiving, attending, understanding, responding, and remembering. Examples are provided to aid each step of the process.

The fourth chapter discusses the five types of listening—informative, relationship, appreciative, critical, and discriminative. Emphasis is given on how to adjust to each listening situation.

The last chapter presents guidelines for effective listening. This discussion covers what we think, how we feel, and what we do about listening. Effective listening has a great deal to do with all of those. I hope this book will help everyone who reads it to become a better listener.

John A. Kline

Acknowledgments

I have studied the listening process extensively and spoken on the subject hundreds of times. And still I am not the effective listener I would like to be. That fact makes writing this book difficult.

Still, I wanted to share what I know about listening. I have done this by using many personal examples and providing numerous explanatory and prescriptive lists. I think you'll find some things to help you be a better listener.

I thank my wife, Ann, and our five grown children, Teri, Marc, Nanette, Missy, and especially our Down's syndrome son David, for teaching me the importance of listening effectively.

Chapter 1

The Need for Better Listening

Listening is the neglected communication skill. While all of us have had instruction in reading, writing, and speaking, few have had any formal instruction in listening. This void in our education is especially interesting in light of research showing that most of us spend seven of every 10 minutes we are awake in some form of communi-

cation activity. Of these seven minutes (or 70 percent of the time we are awake), 10 percent is spent writing, 15 percent reading, 30 percent talking, and 45 percent listening.

Think of it! We spend nearly half of our communication time listening, but few of us make any real effort to be better listeners. For those who do, however, the effort pays great dividends: increased safety, higher productivity, faster learning, and better relationships.

Good listening is important to the Air Force—at times, absolutely crucial! Just how crucial is readily apparent from a report in a USAF air safety publication.* The report presents quotations from a taped conversation between a pilot and a control tower operator during routine landing preparations. The tower operator wants the aircraft to descend from 10 thousand feet to eight thousand feet. Here is that conversation.

TIME	AGENCY	
1929:38	Approach Control:	"Turn right, heading 180. Descend and maintain eight thousand."
1929:42	Aircraft:	"Right 180 out of fifteen thousand for two thousand." (Aircraft's readback was interrupted by another aircraft and not acknowledged by approach control.)
1931:08	Aircraft:	"Steady 180 and passing ten thousand for two thousand."
1931:11	Approach Control:	"Roger."
1931:22	Approach Control:	"Your position 12 miles southwest of airport, maintain eight thousand feet."
1931:30	Aircraft:	"Roger, passing nine for two." (This transmission was not acknowledged by approach control.)
1933:05	Approach Control:	"Your position 19 miles southwest of airport. Turn right 200 for slight pattern extension."

---

*"Hearing But Not Listening," *USAF Aerospace Safety,* January 1971, 8.

The report goes on to say that radar and radio contact was lost "because both crewmen had uttered their final words, victims in a fatal accident of poor listening in the air and on the ground."*

This avoidable accident is but one example in which listening played a crucial role. Effective listening is, in fact, crucial throughout the Air Force. Consider missile crew members who have the capability to unleash weapons of incredible destruction. The primary communication authorizing their launch is an encoded spoken transmission. Consider also command post, security police, and medical personnel who receive information primarily through the spoken word. A simple listening error in any of these areas could result in lost man-hours, equipment, or lives.

Now consider the fact that poor listening is costly in even the most routine staff communications and office operations. Directives to a staff or instructions to office

---

*"Hearing But Not Listening," *USAF Aerospace Safety*, January 1971, 8.

personnel are often given only once. The greater the difference in rank between those giving the directives or instructions and those receiving them, the less inclined the receivers are to ask for clarification—lest they be considered dull, slow, or inattentive. It is important to listen carefully the first time.

Surveys show that Air Force managers put a premium on good listening. Strong listening skills consistently rank at or near the top of characteristics they desire in their subordinates.

Nor are Air Force managers unique in this regard. Far from it—business organizations with a profit motive have long recognized the value of listening effectively. Chief executive officers and chief operating officers of companies large and small say that poor listening is the number one problem in their organizations. Furthermore, they declare that listening is the communication skill most crucial to success. Their comments provoke no surprise, since many formal studies have resulted in the same conclusions: Listening is crucial in the workplace.

But listening is also important in other places—in the home, at church, in civic clubs, and at social gatherings. In these and other places, listening to gain information may be less important than listening to improve relationships. Counselors and other experts on interpersonal communication tell us that listening is the skill that can make or break a relationship. To a certain extent, this type of listening is important in the workplace as well; after all, we humans are relational individuals and it is sometimes as important to understand the person as what the person is saying. Even at work, then, there is a lot more to listening than just understanding the meaning of words.

There is no question but that listening is both crucial and neglected. It is therefore this book's purpose to help you develop better listening skills. The chapters that follow are designed to help you become a better listener in all communication situations. The first step in becoming a better listener is to recognize certain false notions that many people hold about listening. Recognizing these fallacies will help you to avoid being trapped by them.

Chapter 2

Fallacies about Listening

Among the great hindrances to effective listening are the fallacies that people hold about listening. These false ideas often cause people to have inflated opinions of their own listening performance. Believing that they have no problem with listening, they make no effort to improve. Indeed, why should they? Not knowing that their listening skill is "broke," they see no need to "fix" it. Consequently, they don't take steps to improve. Knowing about these fallacies will assist you in avoiding this trap. Here, then, are several of the common ones.

Fallacy #1: Listening Is Not *My* Problem!

People generally believe they are better listeners than those around them. It is the people they work for, the ones who work with or for them, their family members, and their friends who have a problem in listening effectively—not them.

When I teach classes or lead seminars on communication, I often ask participants to assess themselves as listeners. With 10 being high and one being low, they are to rate themselves as listeners compared to the other members of the group. The average score through the years has been about 7.5—some higher, some lower, but the overall average is 7.5.

Next, they rate the other group members as listeners. That rating has been 4.1 on average. In other words, they believe that listening is a problem, but that the problem belongs to someone else. Remember that each group member is being rated as part of the group by the others; that is, each member is part of the group receiving the 4.1 rating.

5

The point is simply this. The people around us believe that we have more of a problem listening effectively than they do. This should tell us something. Listening is not just someone else's problem—it's ours.

Fallacy #2: Listening and Hearing Are the Same

Simply having good hearing does not make one a good listener. In fact, many people who have perfectly good hearing are not good listeners. Having good hearing does facilitate one's perception of sound; but good listeners don't simply hear words—they focus on the meaning. We communicate effectively with each other insofar as we share meaning.

If I tell you something and you misunderstand me, effective communication has not occurred. If I tell you something and you understand what I meant—that is, if we have an effective transfer or sharing of meaning—we say that the communication is effective. Effective listening implies that the listener understands what the speaker means.

The difference between hearing and listening can be stated this way: Hearing is the reception of sound, listening is the attachment of meaning to the sound. Hearing is passive, listening is active. Understanding the difference between hearing and listening is an important prerequisite for listening effectively.

Fallacy #3: Good Readers Are Good Listeners

This statement is often untrue, even though both reading and listening depend on the translation of words into meaning. Because of the shared translation function, there is obviously some kind of relationship between reading and listening; the problem is, many people mistakenly believe that all good readers are necessarily good listeners.

Researchers who administer different standard reading tests to the same individual find a high positive correlation between the two sets of scores; that is, persons who score well on one reading test generally score well on another while persons who score low on one test tend to score low on another.

Similar results are found by researchers who test individuals on standardized listening tests. Those who score high on one test tend to score high on another, and vice versa. Interestingly, however, there is often a surprisingly low correlation between one's scores on reading tests and that same person's scores on listening tests. For a demonstration of this result, consider the following experiment.

A teacher divides a class into two sections, randomly assigning students until each section has half the stu-

dents. Each new "class" is placed in a new, separate class-room. Each student in one class is given a short paper, told to read it once and then place it on the desk, blank side up. Students in the other class listen as the teacher delivers the paper as a speech. Students in both classes are then given identical tests on the material covered.

Experiments like this one consistently result in certain questions being answered correctly more often by those who read the paper while other questions are answered correctly more often by those who heard it delivered as a speech. This result is really not all that surprising. When we read a document, visual cues—margins, illustrations, punctuation—become factors. On the other hand, when we listen, the speaker's vocal emphasis, reading style, pauses, and the like influence our understanding. There is, then, a difference between processing information from the written word and processing it from the spoken word. The fact that some people are better at one than the other demonstrates the fallacy of believing that good readers are necessarily good listeners.

Incidentally, test results also show that most people score higher as readers than as listeners. Being a good reader is no guarantee that you are a good listener.

Fallacy #4: Smarter People Are Better Listeners

Obviously, intelligence plays a role in a person's capacity to listen. Persons with limited intelligence will be limited in their capacity to process the information contained in messages they receive. Conversely, those having high intelligence levels will possess a greater processing capacity. Yet, the belief that "smarter people are better listeners" is often false. In fact, evidence suggests that the reverse is often true.

Some years ago, I administered a listening test and a standardized IQ test to students in several college classes. I compared the results of the listening test to the IQ scores for each student. There was little correlation between listening test results and IQ scores—with one surprising exception: There was an inverse relationship between listening scores and IQ scores for those students having the very highest IQ scores. In other words, the smartest students actually scored lower on the listening test than did many students having lower IQ scores. These results lead to the conclusion that higher intelligence levels do not necessarily result in better listening among college students who possess the capacity—if not always the willingness—to listen. Further, higher intelligence may actually interfere with the listening of those who are the very smartest.

We must keep in mind that this study was conducted with a specific group—college students. Most were in their late teens and early twenties. And the test did not assess all types of listening. It required that students listen to conversations for two reasons: to gain information and to understand something about the speaker—what we will later refer to as informative listening and relationship listening.

It is quite possible that the smarter students were bored with this test. If so, boredom could explain their lower performance. Whatever the reasons, however, the fact remains that smarter people are not necessarily better listeners.

Fallacy #5: Listening Improves with Age

Certainly, the capacity or ability to listen and attach appropriate meaning to messages improves with age and experience—at least in the early years and at least to some point. But although listening *ability* increases, listening *performance* generally declines at some point. But this doesn't have to be the case. The discrepancy between listening ability and listening performance is often due to our having learned bad listening habits. Here are some of the most common bad habits.

1. *Learning not to listen.* We learn a lot about not listening while growing up. For example, a parent tells us: "Don't forget to wear your coat to school!" But we don't want to wear a coat, so we "learn" to not listen. Later, at school, the teacher repeats an assignment several times, hoping to make certain that all the students have heard it. The teacher's behavior reinforces not listening, since there will be multiple opportunities for us to get the information. Another example is found in the focus given to repetition in radio and television advertising. This repetition further conditions us against listening carefully the first time.

2. *Thinking about what we are going to say rather than listening to the speaker.* In trying to plan our response, we often miss the point that the other person is making. Then, when we do talk, it sounds as if we weren't listening—which is exactly what happened.

3. *Talking when we should be listening.* Our entire culture seems to condition us to talk, not to listen. The silent act of listening seems no match for the messages hurled at us almost incessantly. The way to control things—to have things go our way—seems to be by out-talking others. Some justify this behavior by saying, "the squeaky

wheel gets the grease." But the truth of the matter is that we miss a lot by talking when we should be listening. A wise person once observed that since we were created with one mouth and two ears, we should spend twice as much time listening as talking. More of us should heed this advice.

4. *Hearing what we expect to hear rather than what is actually said.* This habit seems to become an increasingly greater problem as we grow older, as suggested by the following incident.

When my youngest daughter, Missy, was in grade school, she frequently invited girlfriends home with her to eat supper and spend the night. And since we had four other children in the household at the time, an extra one or two didn't really bother us. One Saturday, because we were planning to have special guests for the evening meal, I told Missy not to ask anyone home that evening.

"Alright," she answered. Then, "Could I go to Angie's house this afternoon?"

"I guess so," I said, "if it's alright with Angie's mother. But make certain that you are home by five o'clock."

I didn't think about Missy again until about four that afternoon when the phone rang. I answered it and heard the voice on the other end say, "Hello, Daddy. This is Missy."

I was amused that she called me Daddy and then identified herself, but I decided to play along. "Missy who?" I asked.

"The Missy that lives at your house," she said impatiently. "I'd like to talk to Mama."

"Mama's pretty busy," I informed her. "You'll have to talk to me."

"I'd a whole lot rather talk to Mama," she replied.

With all the parental authority I could muster, I told her, "You will have to talk to me."

There was a slight pause, then I heard, "Would it be OK for Angie to eat supper and spend the night with us?"

I exploded! "Missy, didn't I tell you that you were not to ask anybody for tonight? I'm coming to get you right now."

"But, Daddy," she pleaded, "it's only four and you said I could stay till five. And besides. . . ."

I cut her off. "Besides, nothing. I'm coming now. You be ready!"

I was met at the door by Missy and Angie along with Angie's mother, who said, "John, would it be alright for Missy to eat supper and spend the night with us?"

"Why, that would be nice," I replied.

"But Daddy," Missy piped in, "that's what I just asked you and you told me I couldn't."

"Oh, . . . Missy," I stammered. "I thought you were asking if Angie could come to our house."

"It's OK," Missy said. "Sometimes you don't listen very well."

Hearing what we expect rather than what the other person means can pose a big problem. Whether we are listening to learn, evaluate, discriminate, relax, or improve a relationship, it's important to *listen* to the other person.

5. *Not paying attention*. The name of this bad habit says it all. In addition to the bad habits discussed above, there are some other common factors that cause us to not pay attention.

Preoccupation. Sometimes we don't listen because we are preoccupied. We have so many things to think about. Our mind is full of ideas, facts, worries. We are unable to put them aside while we listen. Nevertheless, good listening *demands* that we avoid preoccupation when someone is speaking to us.

Prejudice. Attitudes and feelings not tempered by logical thinking can lead to prejudice. Perhaps we don't like the speaker. Or the subject may be one that we know little about and "don't want to know." Maybe we don't like the method of presentation. In any event, we are prejudiced against the presentation; we have prejudged it. Consequently, we may mentally argue with the speaker. Or we may simply "tune out." Prejudicial thinking can divert our attention away from what the speaker is saying.

Self-centeredness. Since we live with ourselves all day every day, most of us spend much more time thinking about ourselves than about others. It is therefore not surprising that self-concern interferes with our listening to what another is saying. We must work at transferring our concentration from "I" to "You"—from ourselves to the person doing the talking.

Stereotyping. As thinking and feeling human beings, we hold certain beliefs about a variety of subjects. We have "fixed" judgments or concepts which we believe to be true and correct. If a speaker presents evidence that contradicts our beliefs, we tend to ignore what is being said—either because it is not believable to us or because we don't want our ideas challenged. Good listeners do not allow themselves to be trapped by stereotypes.

Fallacy #6: Listening Skills Are Difficult to Learn

Actually, the skills themselves are not all that difficult—and initial progress is rapid. But learning to apply the skills consistently does take hard work. And becoming really proficient takes much time and practice—a lifetime to be exact. But the effort is definitely worthwhile. The last chapter will tell you how to become a better listener in any situation. First, however, we need to understand the process of listening and the types of listening. The next chapter explains the process.

Chapter 3

The Process of Listening

We said earlier that the first step in listening effectively is to recognize certain fallacies or false notions. The next step is to understand the process.

Listening is a complex process—an integral part of the total communication process, albeit a part often ignored. This neglect results largely from two factors.

First, speaking and writing (the sending parts of the communication process) are highly visible, and are more easily assessed than listening and reading (the receiving parts). And reading behavior is assessed much more frequently than listening behavior; that is, we are more often tested on what we read than on what we hear. And when we are tested on material presented in a lecture, generally the lecture has been supplemented by readings.

Second, many of us aren't willing to improve our listening skills. Much of this unwillingness results from our incomplete understanding of the process—and understanding the process could help show us how to improve. To understand the listening process, we must first define it.

Through the years, numerous definitions of listening have been proposed. Perhaps the most useful one defines listening as the process of receiving, attending, and understanding auditory messages; that is, messages transmitted through the medium of sound. Often, the steps of responding and remembering are also included. The process might be diagrammed as shown in figure 1.

The process moves through the first three steps—receiving, attending, understanding—in sequence. Responding and/or remembering may or may not follow. For example, it may be desirable for the listener to respond immediately or to remember the message in order to respond at a later time.

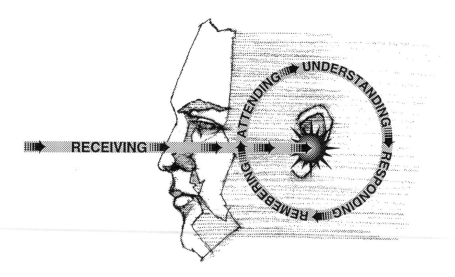

Figure 1. The Listening Process

At times, of course, no response (at least no verbal response) is required. And the act of remembering may or may not be necessary. For example, if someone tells you to "watch your step," you have no need to remember the message after you have completed that step.

Let's look at the parts—the three necessary ones and the two additional ones—one at a time. Consider the following analogy between the listening process and the electronic mail (E-mail) system. Suppose that you are the sender of a message and I am the intended recipient.

Receiving

This step is easily understood. You may send a message to me by E-mail. It may be wonderfully composed and clear. You may have used effective techniques to organize and support your message. The subject may be one of great interest to me. Imagine further that I both admire and respect you, and that I like to receive E-mail from you.

In short, you have done a good job and I want to receive the message. But if I don't turn on my computer, I won't

receive it. The message remains somewhere between your computer and mine—between sender and receiver.

Much human listening fails for the same reason. Receivers simply are not connected or "tuned in" to the senders. Sometimes, the problem is a physiological one; for example, the receiver has a hearing deficiency due to a congenital or inherited weakness. Or perhaps the deficiency resulted from an accident, a disease, or prolonged exposure to loud noises.

Sometimes the problem can be corrected through the use of mechanical devices that restore hearing loss, or through hearing aids that amplify sound. Scientists and engineers are constantly developing new products designed to correct and help specific types of hearing loss.

Remember that hearing and listening are not the same. Hearing is the reception of sound; listening is the attachment of meaning. Hearing is, however, a necessary prerequisite for listening and an important component of the listening process.

Attending

Let's continue with the E-mail analogy. When I turn my computer on, it will receive the message that you sent. But I must do more: I must attend to the message if the process is to continue. Perhaps I received a phone call just after I turned my computer on and had to move away from my desk; I do not know that you have sent a message. Or maybe I don't have an opportunity to read my E-mail that day.

Suppose that I am working on something else when the message arrives. My computer signals that I have mail from you. I want to read it, but I decide that I will do it later. I continue to stay busy on another task, however, and forget to read the message. Later, I may mistakenly "trash it" without ever reading it. Whatever the case, I don't attend to the message.

Human listening is often ineffective—or does not occur—for similar reasons. Receiving occurs, but attending does not.

At any given time, numerous messages compete for our attention. The stimuli may be external, such as words spoken by a lecturer or printed on paper, or events occurring around us. Or the stimuli may be internal, such as a deadline we must meet tomorrow, a backache we developed by sitting too long at the computer, or the hunger pangs we experience because we didn't take time to eat lunch. Whatever the source of the stimuli, we simply can't focus on all of them at the same time. We therefore must choose, whether consciously or unconsciously, to attend to some stimuli and reject others. Three factors determine how these choices are made.

1. *Selectivity of attention.* We direct attention to certain things to prevent an information overload. A common ex-

ample makes the point. Suppose you are attempting to read a book and watch TV at the same time. Although some people claim they can do this, actually both activities suffer—and usually one more than the other. The material that is most engaging or interesting will attract your attention. At other times, something may interrupt or disturb your attention.

In 1974, I was teaching at a large midwestern university. The fad of "streaking"—in which a stark-naked (or nearly naked) student dashes through a gathering of people—had hit the campus. One day as I was lecturing to a thousand students in an auditorium, a streaker dressed only in combat boots and a football helmet ran across the stage. Needless to say, I lost the attention of the audience. I tried for several minutes to regain their attention, then finally decided to dismiss the class 10 minutes early. I had always believed that I was a good lecturer and could hold the audience's attention, no matter what; I was wrong!

Selectivity of attention explains why you "perk up" or pay attention when something familiar to you, such as your hometown or your favorite hobby, is mentioned. In fact, you may have been listening intently to a conversation when someone in a different conversation mentions your name. Immediately, the focus of your attention shifts to the conversation in which your name was mentioned.

2. *Strength of attention.* Attention is not only selective; it possesses energy, or strength. Attention requires effort and desire. In the example of reading a book and watching TV, the receiver (reader/watcher) directed his or her primary attention toward either the book or the TV. Complete attention can be given to only one stimulus at a time, and necessary attention to only a limited number of stimuli at the same time. If we spend too much energy on too many stimuli, we soon will not be paying attention to any of them. We are all familiar with aircraft accidents that were caused at least in part by controllers in the tower having to process too much information.

Consider also how we can be so attentive to a newspaper, a TV program, a personal computer, a sports event, or another individual that we are oblivious to things around us. Watch a young couple in love sometime: You'll see a good example of intensity, or strength of attention.

Still another measure of attention strength is the length of time that the memory of something continues to influence us. I still remember vividly the baptism of my first grandchild, the first major league baseball game I attended, and the first time I kissed my wife—not necessarily in that order, of course. Strength of attention is important.

3. *Sustainment of attention.* Just as attention is determined by selectivity and strength, it is affected by time of sustainment. Our attention wanes, and this fact is important to an understanding of listening.

For example, we can listen to some public speakers far longer than we can listen to others. Duration may depend on the subject, the setting, the way the speech is packaged, and on the speaker's delivery. But no matter how articulate and skilled the speaker, or how interesting the content, our attention finally ends. If for no other reason, the human body requires sleep or attention to other bodily needs. The mind can only pay attention for as long as the body can sit still.

Selectivity, strength, and sustainment determine attention. Receiving and attending are prerequisites to the rest of the listening process. The third step in that process is understanding.

Understanding

Someone has said, "Communication begins with understanding." How true! A message may have been sent and received, and the receiver may have attended to the message—yet, there has been no effective communication. Effective communication depends on understanding; that is, effective communication does not take place until the receiver *understands* the message. Understanding must result for communication to be effective.

Let's return to the E-mail analogy. Suppose I received the E-mail message, "opened" it, and read it. Has effective communication occurred? Not necessarily. Even though I read every word of your message, I may not have understood what you meant.

There are several possible reasons for the misunderstanding. Perhaps I expected the message to say something that it didn't say; my understanding of it may therefore be more in line with my own expectations than what it actually said. We often hear or read what we expect rather than what was actually said or written. (As was illustrated by the story about my daughter, Missy, in the preceding chapter.)

Or perhaps the real point of the message was "tucked away," obscured by several other tidbits of information. And I missed the point. In listening, the key point is sometimes missed. A worker may tell a supervisor several things that happened while the supervisor was out of the office. While relating all the events, the worker mentions that the boss asked that the supervisor call upon his return. The supervisor missed this important piece of information because he was not "ready" for it; that is, he was trying to understand the other parts of the message. Later, he asks the worker why he had failed to tell him that his boss wanted to see him. But the worker *had* told him; he just didn't understand.

Our expectations and/or our failure to get the point often lead to misunderstanding. But the major reason for my not understanding the E-mail I received from you was probably something else: the words you used and the manner in which you arranged them. Neither of us was necessarily "at fault"; we simply attached different meanings to the words. You attached one meaning to those words, I attached another. We communicate effectively with each other only insofar as we share meanings for the symbols—verbal or nonverbal—that we are using.

With E-mail, the message is limited to words or other visual symbols that represent words. In listening, both verbal and nonverbal symbols are crucial to understanding. Consider the roles they play.

1. *Verbal symbols*. Verbal communication means communicating through the use of words, whether spoken or

21

written. Two barriers obstruct our understanding of verbal communication.

Barrier #1: The same words mean different things to different people. This barrier is a common one, and it may be experienced whenever any two people attempt to communicate.

I may tell my colleague that the temperature in the office is quite comfortable. My "quite comfortable," however, is her "uncomfortable": 75 degrees is comfortable for me; 70 degrees is comfortable for her. The same word can mean different things to different people. A friend tells me he will be over in five minutes. To him, five minutes means "soon"—perhaps any time in the next half hour. I, on the other hand, attach a literal meaning: Five minutes means five minutes.

Some years ago, I was speaking at a civilian university. My wife, Ann, had accompanied me and had gone shopping while I was speaking. I had asked her to pick me up at noon. There was an attractive circular drive at the front of the building where I was speaking. To the rear of the building was a small circular drive used mostly by service and delivery vehicles. In my message to Ann, I had said simply, "Pick me up at the circular drive." Ann immediately thought of the nice drive in front of the building; I was thinking of the one at the back. Fortunately, it didn't take us too long to discover the mistake.

In the previous examples, the same words having different meanings for different people caused only minor irritation. The consequences can be more severe, as described in the following story told by a fire inspector.

The fire inspector said that workers exhibit great caution when they are working around gasoline drums. They take great care not to smoke or ignite matches nearby. But when the drums are emptied, and labeled "empty gasoline drums," caution is thrown to the wind. Workers feel comfortable in striking matches and smoking cigarettes in the area. Ironically, vapors that emanate from "empty" drums are much more volatile than liquid gasoline.

The word "empty" holds a different meaning for the workers than for the experienced fire inspector, who knows that the potential for disaster is present. The next example shows how a misunderstanding of one word's meaning can lead to tragic consequences.

A traveler stopped at a convenience store to ask directions. The man behind the counter pointed to a traffic signal a block away and said, "Go to that intersection, take an immediate left, go about a mile. It will be the big red building on your right."

The traveler repeated, "Go to the traffic light, take an immediate left, go a mile to the red building on my right. Is that it?"

"That's right," said the convenience store operator.

Unfortunately, the traffic light was on the corner heading into the intersection and the man in the store had neglected to mention the grassy median that separated northbound and southbound lanes. The traveler took an "immediate left" and headed south in the northbound lane. Less than one block later, he slammed headfirst into an eighteen-wheeler and was killed.

When the same words mean different things to different people, misunderstanding occurs. But there is another barrier to effective verbal communication that can cause just as much trouble.

Barrier #2: Different words sometimes mean the same thing. Many things are called by more than one name. For example, when my adolescent son, Marc, and I went to a restaurant in the South shortly after we had moved here from the Midwest, Marc asked the waiter to bring him a "pop." The waiter didn't understand until Marc said, "You know—pop, it comes in a bottle or a can; you shake it and it fizzes." The waiter said, "Oh! You mean a soda." But "soda" meant quite something else to Marc, and there were a few more moments of confusion until the waiter and Marc understood one another. Soft drink, soda, and pop all mean the same thing when used in the same context. The name used depends on who is doing the talking. How many things in the English language are called by more than one name? For a starter, consider that the 500 most commonly used words in our language have a total of about 15,000 definitions—an average of 30 per word. The following sentence will serve to illustrate the point.

> Fred has been crestfallen since he fell out of favor with the Fall Festival Committee last fall after he had a falling out with Joe because Joe had fallen in with a new crowd of people rather than falling in love with Fred's sister, Fallina.

Not a great sentence, but it illustrates a few of the more than 50 meanings of "fall." Our language is marked by its multiusage. If you doubt it, describe some object or animal in detail to several talented artists and ask them to draw what you describe. Chances are that each one will draw a distinctively different picture.

These two barriers—same words meaning different things and different words meaning the same thing—can be overcome if you realize the following fact: *Meanings are not in words, meanings are in people.* We listen more effectively when we consider the message in relation to its source. Good listeners always consider who the sender of the message is. Knowing something about the sender pays big dividends when it comes to understanding the message.

2. *Nonverbal symbols.* We use nonverbal symbols to transmit many times more information than our verbal symbols carry. We communicate nonverbally through action factors, nonaction factors, and vocal factors. Each suggests a barrier to listening.

Barrier #1: Misinterpretation of the action. Eye contact, gestures, and facial expression are action factors that affect the meaning we attach to a message. For that matter, any movement or action carries meaning.

When someone walks quickly away from a conversation or taps a pencil on the desk during a conversation, we may conclude that the person is in a hurry or is bored. Our conclusions may or may not be correct, however. We may conclude that speakers who twitch, or otherwise seem to us unsure, are nervous when, in fact, they may not be.

Barrier #2: Misinterpretation of nonaction symbols. The clothes I wear, the automobile I drive, and the objects in my office—all these things communicate something about me. In addition, my respect of your needs for time and space affects how you interpret my messages. For example, if I am to see you at noon but arrive 15 minutes late, my tardiness may affect how you interpret what I say to you. Or if I "crowd" you—get too "close" to you emotionally—when speaking, you may "tune me out"; that is, you may "hear" but not "listen to" my message.

Barrier #3: Misinterpretation of the voice. The quality, intelligibility, and variety of the voice affect the listener's understanding. Quality refers to the overall impression the voice makes on others. Listeners often infer from the voice whether the speaker is happy or sad, fearful or confident, excited or bored. Intelligibility (or understandability) depends on such things as articulation, pronunciation, and grammatical correctness. But variety is the spice of speaking. Variations in rate, volume, force, pitch, and emphasis are some of the factors that influence our understanding of the speaker's message.

Receiving, attending, and understanding are all crucial if effective listening is to occur, for communication can accurately be defined as the sharing or understanding of meaning. Often, however, the steps of responding and remembering are part of the listening process. Responding and remembering are indicators of listening accuracy.

Responding

The listening process may end with understanding, since effective communication and effective listening may be defined as the accurate sharing or understanding of meaning. But a response may be needed—or at least helpful. And there are different types of responses.

1. *Direct verbal responses*. These may be spoken or written. Let's continue with the E-mail analogy. After I have received, attended to, and understood the message you sent, I may respond verbally. If your message asked a

question or sought my coordination, I might type a response on my computer and reply to you. Perhaps you requested that I call you or come to see you, in which case I do so. Or you might have asked me to write a position paper or think about an issue and give you some advice, in which case I might send a quick E-mail response indicating that I will get back to you later.

2. *Responses that seek clarification.* I may use E-mail to ask for additional information, or I may talk to you either on the telephone or face-to-face. I may be very direct in my request, or I may just say, "tell me more about it."

3. *Responses that paraphrase.* I may say something like, "in other words, what you are saying is. . . ." A paraphrase gives the sender a chance to agree, or to provide information to clarify the message.

4. *Nonverbal responses.* Many times, a nonverbal response is all that is needed; indeed, it may even be the preferred type of response. The knowing nod of the head, an understanding smile, or a "thumbs up" may communicate that the message is understood.

Responding, then, is a form of feedback that completes the communication transaction. It lets the sender know that the message was received, attended to, and understood.

Remembering

Memorization of facts is not the key to good listening. Yet memory is often a necessary and integral part of the listening process. Some would go so far as to say, "if you can't remember it, you weren't listening."

This statement is often untrue. Think for example, of the times you heard a good joke but can't remember it long enough to get home and tell it; or the number of times you have gone to the grocery store and couldn't remember what you were asked to buy. And the most frustrating situation of all—you were introduced to someone and can't recall the name five minutes later. We often say, "I can remember faces, but I can't remember names."

At times, something will "jog" our memory, such as hearing another joke, seeing a similar product on the grocery store shelf, or meeting someone else with the same first name.

What is the relationship between memory and listening? Understanding the differences between short-term memory and long-term memory will help explain the relationship.

With short-term memory, information is used immediately—within a few seconds, for example, as with a phone number that we look up. Short-term memory has a rapid forgetting rate and is very susceptible to interruption. And the amount of information that can be retained is quite limited, though it varies somewhat with variations in the material to be retained. For example, most of us can remember only very few random numbers (4, 13, 9, 53, 274, 6, 491, 713, 2810, 1, 7555, 111). But if there is a pattern (1, 2, 4, 8, 16, 32, 64, 128, 256, 512, 1024, 2048), the task is much easier.

Long-term memory allows us to recall information and events hours, days, weeks—even years—later. You remember, for example, things that happened to you when you were growing up, songs you learned, people you knew. You may have been unaware of those memories for long periods of time, and then the right stimulus caused you to recall them. Perhaps the aroma of a freshly baked pie called to mind your grandmother, who used to make great apple pies years ago.

The next chapter discusses the five basic types of listening; chapter 5 tells how you can be a better listener in different types of situations.

Chapter 4

Types of Listening

Different situations require different types of listening. We may listen to obtain information, improve a relationship, gain appreciation for something, make discriminations, or engage in a critical evaluation.

While certain skills are basic and necessary for all types of listening (receiving, attending, and understanding), each type requires some special skills. Chapter 5 dis-

cusses those special skills and presents guidelines to improve listening behavior in all situations. But before we can fully appreciate the skills and apply the guidelines, we must understand the different types of listening.

Informative Listening

Informative listening is the name we give to the situation where the listener's primary concern is to understand the message. Listeners are successful insofar as the meaning they assign to messages is as close as possible to that which the sender intended.

Informative listening, or listening to understand, is found in all areas of our lives. Much of our learning comes from informative listening. For example, we listen to lectures or instructions from teachers—and what we learn depends on how well we listen. In the workplace, we listen to understand new practices or procedures—and how well we perform depends on how well we listen. We listen to instructions, briefings, reports, and speeches; if we listen poorly, we aren't equipped with the information we need.

At times, careful informative listening is crucial—remember the aircraft landing report in chapter 1. At other times, careless listening results in only aggravation or misunderstanding—remember my misunderstanding of my daughter, Missy, as presented in chapter 2. Whatever the case, effective informative listening demands that you concentrate squarely on the message—and know its source.

There are three key variables related to informative listening. Knowing these variables can help you begin to improve your informative listening skills; that is, you will become increasingly successful in understanding what the speaker means.

1. *Vocabulary*. The precise relationship between vocabulary and listening has never been determined, but it is clear that increasing your vocabulary will increase your potential for better understanding. And it's never too late to improve your vocabulary. Having a genuine interest in words and language, making a conscious effort to learn

new words, breaking down unfamiliar words into their component parts—all these things will help you improve your vocabulary.

Another good way to improve your vocabulary is to be sensitive to the context in which words are used. Sometimes, unfamiliar words appear with synonyms: Her attractive, *winsome* personality won us over. At other times, a contrast is drawn: He is usually quite energetic, but today he seemed *lethargic*. Occasionally, an unfamiliar word is used to summarize a situation or quality: He passed for over 200 yards, ran for 50 more, and his three punts averaged over 45 yards; he turned in a *stellar* performance.

Look for these and other contextual clues to help you learn new words and improve your vocabulary.

2. *Concentration.* Concentration is difficult. You can remember times when another person was not concentrating on what you were saying—and you probably can remember times when you were not concentrating on something that someone was saying to you.

Some years ago my oldest daughter, Teri, interrupted my reading of the newspaper to ask, "Is it OK if I take your car over to a friend's house to spend the night? I'll be home before you go to work in the morning." Without concentrating on what she was asking, I said, "Sure, go ahead." Several minutes later, I realized what she had said. She was not coming home that night, and I had to leave the house earlier than usual the next morning. I had to drive from Montgomery to Mobile, where I was to give a speech—and all my notes and visual aids were in my automobile. Fortunately for me, Teri had left the telephone number of her friend, and I was able to retrieve my automobile.

There are many reasons people don't concentrate when listening. Sometimes listeners try to divide their attention between two competing stimuli. At other times, listeners are preoccupied with something other than the speaker of the moment. Sometimes listeners are too ego-involved, or too concerned with their own needs to concentrate on the message being delivered. Or perhaps they lack curiosity,

31

energy, or interest. Many people simply have not learned to concentrate while listening. Others just refuse to discipline themselves, lacking the motivation to accept responsibility for good listening. Concentration requires discipline, motivation, and acceptance of responsibility.

3. *Memory.* Memory is an especially crucial variable to informative listening; you cannot process information without bringing memory into play. More specifically, memory helps your informative listening in three ways.

a. It allows you to recall experiences and information necessary to function in the world around you. In other words, without memory you would have no knowledge bank.

b. It establishes expectations concerning what you will encounter. You would be unable to drive in heavy traffic, react to new situations, or make common decisions in life without memory of your past experiences.

c. It allows you to understand what others say. Without simple memory of the meaning of words, you could not communicate with anyone else. Without memory of concepts and ideas, you could not understand the meaning of messages.

Relationship Listening

The purpose of relationship listening is either to help an individual or to improve the relationship between people. Therapeutic listening is a special type of relationship listening. Therapeutic listening brings to mind situations where counselors, medical personnel, or other professionals allow a troubled person to talk through a problem. But it can also be used when you listen to friends or acquaintances and allow them to "get things off their chests." Although relationship listening requires you to listen for information, the emphasis is on understanding the other person. Three behaviors are key to effective relationship listening: attending, supporting, and empathizing.

1. *Attending.* Much has been said about the importance of "paying attention," or "attending" behavior. In relationship listening, attending behaviors indicate that

the listener is focusing on the speaker. Nonverbal cues are crucial in relationship listening; that is, your nonverbal behavior indicates that you are attending to the speaker— or that you aren't!

Eye contact is one of the most important attending behaviors. Looking appropriately and comfortably at the speaker sends a message that is different from that sent by a frequent shift of gaze, staring, or looking around the room. Body positioning communicates acceptance or lack of it. Leaning forward, toward the speaker, demonstrates interest; leaning away communicates lack of interest. Head nods, smiles, frowns, and vocalized cues such as "uh huh," "I see," or "yes"—all are positive attending behaviors. A pleasant tone of voice, gentle touching, and concern for the other person's comfort are other attending behaviors.

2. *Supporting.* Many responses have a negative or nonsupportive effect; for example, interrupting the speaker, changing the subject, turning the conversation toward yourself, and demonstrating a lack of concern for the other person. Giving advice, attempting to manipulate the conversation, or indicating that you consider yourself superior are other behaviors that will have an adverse effect on the relationship.

Sometimes the best response is silence. The speaker may need a "sounding board," not a "resounding board." Wise relationship listeners know when to talk and when to just listen—and they generally listen more than they talk.

Three characteristics describe supportive listeners: (1) discretion—being careful about what they say and do; (2) belief—expressing confidence in the ability of the other person; and (3) patience—being willing to give others the time they need to express themselves adequately.

3. *Empathizing.* What is empathy? It is not sympathy, which is a feeling for or about another. Nor is it apathy, which is a lack of feeling. Empathy is feeling and thinking *with* another person. The caring, empathic listener is able to go into the world of another—to see as the other sees, hear as the other hears, and feel as the other feels.

33

Obviously, the person who has had more experience and lived longer stands a better chance of being an effective empathic listener. The person who has never been divorced, lost a child to death, been bankrupt, or lost a job may have a more difficult time relating to people with these problems than one who has experienced such things.

Risk is involved with being an empathic relationship listener. You cannot be an effective empathic listener without becoming involved, which sometimes means learning more than you really want to know. But commanders can't command effectively, bosses can't supervise skillfully, and individuals can't relate interpersonally without empathy. Abraham Lincoln is reported to have said, "I feel sorry for the man who cannot feel the stripes upon the back of another." Truly, those who cannot feel *with* another person are at a disadvantage in understanding that person.

Empathic behavior can be learned. First, you must learn as much as you can about the other person. Second, you must accept the other person—even if you can't accept some aspects of that person's behavior. Third, you must have the desire to be an empathic listener. And you must remember that empathy is crucial to effective relationship listening.

Appreciative Listening

Appreciative listening includes listening to music for enjoyment, to speakers because you like their style, to your choices in theater, television, radio, or film. It is the response of the listener, not the source of the message, that defines appreciative listening. That which provides appreciative listening for one person may provide something else for another. For example, hard rock music is not a source of appreciative listening for me. I would rather listen to gospel, country, jazz, or the "golden oldies."

The quality of appreciative listening depends in large part on three factors: presentation, perception, and previous experience.

1. *Presentation.* I just mentioned that I prefer gospel music to hard rock. But I don't enjoy *all* gospel. For example, I don't enjoy gospel music when it is presented in a "glitzy" setting—or when it is performed by someone who fails to demonstrate an understanding of the music's meaning. (I might add that I don't usually enjoy gospel when it is off-key or poorly done—but there are exceptions, such as the time I heard a 103-year-old man sing "Amazing Grace." Never have I enjoyed it more!)

I enjoy gospel music when I hear it in the little churches of rural Alabama. I also enjoy it when it is presented in the large church I attend in Montgomery. I also very much enjoy presentations of gospel music on radio, on television, or in concert by well-known performers who understand its meaning.

I enjoy hearing good speakers, speakers whom I admire, and speakers who have expertise. I frequently attend lectures at Air University by speakers who have all three of these characteristics. Among the speakers I have heard there recently: General Charles "Chuck" Horner, the air component commander of Desert Storm—a war dominated by airpower; Deputy Secretary of Defense, Dr John White; former Chairman of the Joint Chiefs of Staff, General Colin Powell; and US Ambassador to the UN, Jeanne Kirkpatrick. I have heard many other outstanding speakers at Air University, of course—these four simply came to mind readily as examples of speakers who had all three of the characteristics mentioned above: all were good speakers; all had my admiration; and all had a great deal of expertise.

Presentation encompasses many factors: the medium, the setting, the style and personality of the presenter, to name just a few. Sometimes it is our perception of the presentation, rather than the actual presentation, that most influences our listening pleasure or displeasure. Perception is an important factor in appreciative listening.

2. *Perception.* For years, I did not care to listen to jazz music. I had always believed that people like me—from a conservative rural midwestern background—wouldn't like jazz. Then I started to work for a new boss—a general officer who enjoyed jazz. I admired him very much. My

mind was now open to listen to jazz. My perception was changing, and I began to enjoy jazz music.

Expectations play a large role in perception. If I attend a concert under duress with no expectation of enjoying the music (perhaps my wife insists that I attend, or my position in the community makes it the thing to do), I may be pleasantly surprised. But I stand a lot better chance of enjoying the concert if I *expect* to enjoy it.

Perceptions—and the expectations that drive them—have their basis in attitudes. Our attitudes determine how we react to, and interact with, the world around us. There was a time, not many years ago, when I did not want a personal computer (PC) in my office. I did not want to even be *around* a PC. I did not enjoy working with computers.

Six years ago, I wrote a book called *Speaking Effectively: A Guide for Air Force Speakers.** The book you are now reading is a companion volume to that one. I wrote the first book in longhand; I'm composing this one on my PC. Fortunately for me, my attitude toward computers has changed. If my attitude had changed six years sooner, I could have written the earlier book in less time—and saved both time and effort for the publisher.

Perceptions influence all areas of our lives. Certainly, they are crucial determinants as to whether or not we enjoy or appreciate the things we listen to. Obviously, perceptions also determine what we listen to in the first place. As we said earlier, listening is selective.

3. *Previous experience.* The discussion of perception makes it clear that previous experience influences whether we enjoy listening to something. In some cases, we enjoy listening to things because we are experts in the area. Sometimes, however, expertise or previous experience prevents us from enjoying a presentation because we are too sensitive to imperfections. Previous experience plays a large role in appreciative listening.

Many people enjoy the sounds of large-city traffic. Perhaps their growing up in a large city was a happy experience for them. The blare of horns honking, the sound of roaring engines accelerating, even the shrill shriek of sirens piercing the air—all these things may remind them of pleasant times in their lives. They appreciate hearing these sounds.

Others, having grown up on a farm or in a small town, have learned to enjoy the sounds of nature. For them, a walk in the country produces sounds of enjoyment: the rustle of leaves in the breeze, the song of a robin, the babble of a brook.

Usually, if we associate a sound or other experience with pleasant memories, then we appreciate or enjoy it. However, if the sound or experience is associated with unpleasant memories, we probably will not appreciate or enjoy it.

---

*John A. Kline, *Speaking Effectively* (Maxwell AFB, Ala.: Air University Press, 1989).

But we can change! Let's return to the example of how I learned to enjoy listening to jazz. I did not enjoy jazz music when I first heard it. Then I worked for a man who enjoyed it. More than once when we were TDY, I sat with him in the evenings listening to jazz combos or jazz pianists . . . and I learned to like jazz. We should not shut our minds to the fact that we can learn to like, enjoy, and appreciate new and different things. We can learn to be better appreciative listeners.

Critical Listening

The ability to listen critically is essential in a democracy. On the job, in the community, at service clubs, in places of worship, in the family—there is practically no place you can go where critical listening is unimportant. Politicians, the media, salesmen, advocates of policies and procedures, and our own financial, emotional, intellectual, physical, and spiritual needs require us to place a premium on critical listening and the thinking that accompanies it.

The subject of critical listening deserves much more attention than we can afford it here. But there are three things to keep in mind. These three things were outlined by Aristotle, the classical Greek rhetorician, more than 2,000 years ago in his treatise, *The Rhetoric*.* They are as follows: *ethos*, or speaker credibility; *logos*, or logical arguments; and *pathos*, or psychological appeals.

1. *Ethos*. Credibility of the speaker is important. The two critical factors of speaker credibility are expertness and trustworthiness. A speaker may be expert or competent and still not be trustworthy. For example, an autocratic dictator of a certain third world country might be an expert on the question of his country's possession of nuclear arms; but I would not trust him to tell me. On the other hand a person might be trustworthy, but not be an expert on the subject. I trust my best friend; he would tell me the truth about nuclear arms in that third world country, if he knew and I asked him. But his information would be of questionable validity since he is simply not an expert in such things.

When listening to a message that requires a critical judgment or response, ask yourself, "Is the speaker a credible source, one who is both an expert on the subject and one who can be trusted to be honest, unbiased, straightforward?" Remember that a person may have personality or charisma. But these do not take the place of credibility. A person may even be highly competent and an expert in one area and simply not be informed in another.

Returning to the example of speakers at Air University, I trust General Horner. He is an expert on the use of air-

---

*Aristotle, *Art of Rhetoric* (New York: Viking Penguin, 1992).

power, and he is trustworthy. I listen intently when he speaks on the subject. But I would not expect him to be an expert on buying used cars, knitting, or nutrition. He may be an expert on any or all of these things, but I would want to "check it out" before I put too much stock in his ideas on these subjects.

Effective critical listening requires careful judgment about the expertness and trustworthiness of the speaker. In fact, ethos or speaker credibility may be the most important single factor in critical listening and thinking. However, ethos without logos is not enough.

2. *Logos.* Even speakers with high ethos often make errors in logic, not by intention, but by accident, carelessness, inattention to detail, or lack of analysis. Critical listeners have a right to expect well supported arguments from speakers, arguments that contain both true propositions and valid inferences or conclusions.

When evaluating arguments, listeners should ask several questions about the proposition or statements made:

   a. Are the statements true?
   b. Are the data the best that can be obtained?
   c. Are the sources of the data known to the listeners? In other words do listeners know where the information came from?
   d. Is the data accurately portrayed?
   e. Is the data representative? That is, would all the data, or at least a preponderance of it show the same thing?

The above questions may all be answered to your satisfaction, yet the logic may be faulty. For perhaps the data do not lead to or justify the inferences or conclusions drawn. Listeners should ask themselves the following questions:

   a. Is the conclusion a certainty or are exceptions possible?
   b. Were all cause-effect relationships established beyond doubt?
   c. Does the data justify the inference drawn or the conclusion given?

d. Does the inference or conclusion "follow" from the data, or is there a *non sequitur*, which means literally, "it does not necessarily follow"?

e. Is there evidence of strong logical thinking by the speaker?*

Both ethos and logos are crucial elements of critical listening. But reliance on just these two elements without consideration of pathos would be akin to attempting to sit on a three-legged stool with one leg missing. Pathos is the third leg.

3. *Pathos.* The psychological or emotional element of communication is often misunderstood and misused. Simply said, speakers often use psychological appeals to gain an emotional response from listeners. Effective critical listeners carefully determine the focus of the speaker's message.

Speakers may appeal to any one or several needs, desires, or values that are important to us including: adventure, thrift, curiosity, fear, creativity, companionship, guilt, independence, loyalty, power, pride, sympathy, altruism. There are many others, of course; the list is a long one.

There are several questions critical listeners should ask themselves when assessing the pathos element:

a. Is the speaker attempting to manipulate rather than persuade me?

b. What is the speaker's intent?

c. Is the speaker combining logos with pathos?

d. Am I responding merely to the pathos?

e. Next week or next year will I be satisfied with the decision I am making today?

Effective critical listening depends on the listener keeping all three elements of the message in the analysis and in perspective: ethos, or source credibility; logos, or logical argument; and pathos, or psychological appeals.

---

*In *Speaking Effectively* (Maxwell AFB, Ala.: Air University Press, 1989), I discuss the concept of logical thinking in more detail than is given here.

41

Discriminative Listening

The final type of listening is discriminative listening. It may be the most important type, for it is basic to the other four. By being sensitive to changes in the speaker's rate, volume, force, pitch, and emphasis, the informative listener can detect even nuances of difference in meaning. By sensing the impact of certain responses, such as "uh huh," or "I see," relationship listening can be strengthened. Detection of differences between sounds made by certain instruments in the orchestra, or parts sung by the a cappella vocal group, enhances appreciative listening. Finally, sensitivity to pauses, and other vocal and nonverbal cues, allows critical listeners to more accurately judge not only the speaker's message, but his intentions as well.

Obviously, many people have good discriminatory listening ability in some areas but not in others. Our middle daughter, Nanette, has always been very adept at picking up minute differences in a person's voice that might signal feelings. She has a gift for discriminating and applying what she hears to relationship listening. But her ability to discriminate among the different sounds that come from an automobile engine is practically nil. One weekend she pulled into the driveway, fan belt squealing. I said, "Nanette, can't you hear that? You're wearing out a belt. You're lucky you got home." "Oh that," she said. "I wondered what that was. I had no idea."

Although discriminative listening cuts across the other four types of listening, there are three things to consider about this type of listening.

1. *Hearing ability*. Obviously, people who lack the ability to hear well will have greater difficulty in discriminating among sounds. Often this problem is more acute for some frequencies, or pitches, than others. For example, a person may be less able to discriminate when the sound is coming from a bass voice than from a higher pitched one.

2. *Awareness of sound structure*. Native speakers become quite proficient at recognizing vowel and consonant sounds that do or do not appear at the beginning, middle,

or end of words. For example, a listener might hear "this sandal" when what the speaker said was "this handle"; but since English words do not begin with "sb," one would not mistake "this bean" for "this sbean."

Attention to the sound structure of the language will lead to more proficient discriminatory listening. A person who pays attention to sound structure would recognize that a rapidly spoken "Idrankitfirst" could mean either "I drank it first" or "I'd rank it first." Recognition of the two meanings would cause the listener to seek clarification.*

3. *Integration of nonverbal cues.* The previous chapter pointed out how action, nonaction, and vocal factors were important in understanding messages. Nowhere is attention to these factors more important than in effective discriminative listening. Words don't always communicate true feelings. The way they are said, or the way the speaker acts, may be the key to understanding the true or intended meaning.

Effective listening, whether informative, relational, appreciative, critical, or discriminative, requires skill. In some cases, the skills are the same for the various types of listening; in some cases, they are quite different. The next chapter will give you guidelines for better listening. It will also tell you which skills are especially critical for each type of listening.

---

*I am indebted for these examples and other ideas to Andrew Wolvin and Carolyn Gwynn Coakley, *Listening* (Madison, Wis.: Brown and Benchmark, 1996).

Chapter 5

How to Be an Effective Listener

The first four chapters discussed the need for effective listening, fallacies about listening, the process of listening, and the types of listening. They provided the background you need to improve your listening skills. This chapter is a prescriptive one. It offers practical suggestions on how to be a better listener.

While there are many ways to construct a list of suggestions, we will consider them in terms of what works best in three major categories:

1. What you *think* about listening.
2. What you *feel* about listening.
3. What you *do* about listening.

You can learn to listen effectively; look now at the components of that learning: thinking, feeling, doing.

What You *Think* about Listening

Although thinking, feeling, and doing go hand in hand, the thinking (or cognitive) domain of learning is perhaps the best place to begin. After all, effective listening takes effort—it requires maximum thinking power. Here are six suggestions.

1. *Understand the complexities of listening.* Most of us take good listening for granted. Therefore, we don't work very hard at improving. But listening is a complex activity, and its complexity explains the emphasis given in previous chapters to understanding the fallacies, processes, and types of listening.

Knowing the fallacies about listening can keep you from being trapped by them. Knowing that the process involves more than just receiving messages will help you focus on not just receiving, but the other components as well. Rec-

45

ognizing the five major types of listening will help you to consciously direct your energies toward the type of listening required for the circumstance of the moment.

Listening requires an active response, not a passive one. Effective listening doesn't just happen; it takes thought—and thinking can be hard work. But there is no other way to become an effective listener. Think about the complexities of listening, and work to understand them.

2. *Prepare to Listen.* Preparation consists of three phases—long-term, mid-term, and short-term. We said earlier that becoming an effective listener is a lifetime endeavor; in other words, expanding your listening ability will be an ongoing task. But there are two things you can do to improve your listening skills for the long term: (a) practice listening to difficult material and (b) build your vocabulary.

Too many people simply do not challenge their listening ability. Since most of today's radio and television programs do not require concentrated or careful listening, your listening skills do not improve through continued exposure to them. And you have to stretch if you want to grow. Force yourself to listen carefully to congressional debates, lectures, sermons, or other material that requires concentration.

Building your vocabulary will improve your conversational skills and your reading skills as well as your listening skills. And the more words you learn, the better listener you will become.

Mid-term preparation for listening requires that you do the necessary background study before the listening begins. Background papers, prebriefs, and an advance look at a hard copy (or an electronic display) of briefing slides or charts will assist you in being ready to listen.

Short-term preparation may be defined as an immediate readiness to listen. When the speaker's mouth opens, you should open your ears. That is not the time to be hunting for a pen, reading a letter from home, or thinking about some unrelated subject. Good listeners—really good listeners—are in the "spring-loaded position to listen." It is important to *prepare* to listen.

3. *Adjust to the situation.* No listening situation is exactly the same as another. The time, the speaker, the message—all change. But many other variables also affect listening, though less obviously so: physiological variables such as rest, hunger, comfort, endurance; psychological variables such as emotional stability, rapport with the speaker, knowledge of the subject; and physical factors such as size and color of the room. Obviously, some of these things will have a positive effect on your listening while others will have a negative effect.

A thick foreign accent, poor grammar, a room with poor acoustics, and the subject of the previous speaker—all may present special barriers to effective listening. However, being aware of the barriers and thinking about how to overcome them can help you improve the situation.

Good listeners are never trapped into thinking that any communication transaction or listening situation is exactly like any other. The Grecian philosopher Heraclitus said it well: "You can't step into the same stream twice." Things change. By thinking about the unique factors of the situation, you can do your most effective job as a listener. Adjust to the situation!

4. *Focus on ideas or key points.* At times, you may understand the process, you may have prepared well, and you may be able to adjust to the situation—yet you fail as a listener. This failure results because you didn't listen to the right things. For example, you may remember a funny story the speaker told to make a point; but you missed the point.

Others boast, "I listen only for the facts." By concentrating exclusively on individual supporting facts, they may actually miss the main ideas. Facts A, B, and C may be interesting in their own right, but the speaker's reason for offering them is usually to develop a generalization from them. Generalizations, not facts, are usually most important.

In studies conducted some years ago at the University of New Mexico, I discovered that students who did best on all but rote memory examinations were those who listened for key points and ideas. Interestingly, those who attempted to memorize minute details did only slightly better on low-level rote memory exams than the individuals who focused on ideas—and they did much worse when long-term retention was the criterion. While there are some exceptions, as when listening for directions to someone's house or memorizing a mathematical formula, it is usually best to focus on ideas or key points.

5. *Capitalize on the speed differential.* Thought can operate much faster than speech. An average person may speak two or three words a second—120 to 180 words a minute. In bursts of enthusiasm, we may even speak a little faster. Most public speakers speak somewhat slower, especially to large audiences. Yet most listeners can pro-

cess up to 500 words per minute, depending on the nature and difficulty of the material.

I have a machine that compresses speech on tape, but without the distortions normally associated with fast forwarding a tape or simply playing a tape or record at a faster speed. Compression is accomplished through systematic removal of small segments—so small that distortion is not noticed by listeners. Experiments in which listening time is cut in half—an hour lecture is listened to in half the time—reveal little, if any, significant loss in listening and learning. Admittedly, listeners are ready for a break because there is no time for their minds to wander. Effective listening requires hard thinking, especially if the material is challenging.

The results of these experiments point to the possibility of capitalizing on the speed differential. Unfortunately, the differential between speed of thought and speed of speech promotes daydreaming or concentrating on something other than what is being said. This is not the case with good listeners, however; they use the time differential to good advantage. They summarize, anticipate, and formulate questions based on the speaker's message. This type of time usage may explain why top listeners at the Air War College recently reported that they learned more from lectures than from any other method of instruction. They have learned to capitalize on the speed differential.

6. *Organize material for learning.* Obviously, speakers can enhance listening through careful organization and presentation of ideas. And if questions are appropriate, you can seek clarification of any points you fail to understand. Often, however, questioning is not permitted or, perhaps due to time constraints or the size of the audience, is inappropriate. What can you do?

Remembering that the speed differential exists, you can arrange the material in your mind or in your notes as it's being presented. This will help you understand and remember it later. You can prepare yourself to retain the information to be presented by asking these questions: What point is the speaker trying to make? What main ideas should I remember? How does this information relate to what I already know?

Reorganizing the material you need to learn, and seeking relationships between the new material and what you already know, requires concentrated thinking. It is easier to simply "tune out." There was a time in my early college years when I could not, "for the life of me," see the relevance of some required classes to my course of study. A professor for whom I had great respect explained it to me this way: "John, someday you will come to understand that all information is part of a large mosaic or universe of knowledge. When that happens, you will value all learning. Always look for how the information relates to what you already know and what you need to know, and you will always find something." You know what? He was right!

What You *Feel* about Listening

We began by discussing what you think about listening because effective listening requires rigorous cognitive processing, or thought. But possession of the sharpest mind will not make you a good listener if your feelings are wrong. In other words, what you feel about listening is important. Here are six suggestions for improving your "feel" for listening.

1. *Want to listen.* This suggestion is basic to all others, for it simply says that you must have an intent to listen. We can all recall having been forced to listen to a speech or a briefing that we didn't really want to listen to. And listening under duress seldom results in understanding or enjoyment, although there are exceptions. Perhaps you have attended a meeting or a social event out of a sense of duty, yet found it to have been profitable. The reason? Probably, since you were there, you decided to make the best of the situation; that is, you made up your mind to listen.

Sometimes you don't want to listen. At other times, your actions may indicate that you don't want to listen when you really do. And at still other times, you may be unaware that you don't want to listen. All three of these situations are affective or attitudinal; that is, they involve your feelings about listening.

Individuals often stop by my office and ask if they can talk for a few minutes. Perhaps they are seeking advice, telling about a project, or seeking clarification on a directive. Whatever the case, if I am not meeting with someone else or working against a deadline, I invite them in. But I must honestly admit that my mind sometimes wanders and I find myself looking at phone messages, fiddling with a paper clip, or looking at my guest with a blank stare. The visitor usually becomes uneasy, hurries the discussion, and offers to come back another time. I protest that I am really listening, but my actions betray me. It is difficult—indeed, nearly impossible—to really listen if you don't have a mind to. You must *want* to listen.

2. *Delay judgment.* There are times when you must be a critical or judgmental listener. You must weigh the merits of what the speaker is saying. At times, you must make crucial decisions based on what you hear. There are also times when you must judge the speaker. Job interviews, campaign promises, speech contests—all are examples of where judgment of the speaker is important. The problem is, though, that you may be judgmental when you shouldn't be. You may judge the speaker instead of the content, or you may form judgments before the speaker has finished.

A boy who was one month shy of being 16 decided to confess to his father that he had driven the family car on the previous night. His younger sister's promised ride to gymnastics class hadn't arrived, and it was the night of her final rehearsal before a performance. So he made the decision to take her even though he did not yet have a driver's license. He was also quite sure that he hadn't been seen and would never be found out. Still, his conscience was bothering him and his family had stressed honesty and openness. He decided to tell his father.

Upon hearing that the boy had taken the car, his father became furious. He scarcely heard the reason, and he failed to consider that the boy had taken it upon himself to confess. He told the boy that the act would delay his getting a driver's license by two months.

Then the father rethought the situation and said, "Son, I acted hastily. My emotions got the best of me. You were wrong to drive the car because you broke the law. But, frankly, I am proud of you for three reasons: you got your sister to gymnastics rehearsal, you were honest about it, and you are my son."

Supervisors often wonder why people in their organization won't level with them. They need only to consider the messenger in ancient Rome who paid with his life for bringing bad news. An ancient Turkish proverb says, "messenger with bad news should keep one foot in the stirrup." Delaying judgment and judging the content rather than the speaker will lead to better listening and more honest communication.

3. *Admit your biases.* Let's face it: Everyone is human! We all have likes and dislikes; some things turn us on, others turn us off. These characteristics are natural and to be expected. The problem comes when we let our biases—our likes and dislikes—get in the way of understanding the speaker's message.

For example, suppose you have had three bad experiences with people from Chicago and you learn that the speaker you have come to hear is from Chicago. You may have a tendency to immediately distrust him, or to discredit whatever he has to say. Only by admitting your prejudice against people from Chicago will you be able to think beyond your past experience and listen effectively to what this speaker has to say.

Before you reject the above example as irrelevant, consider a time in your past when you got sick after eating a certain food. You knew the sickness was caused by a virus and not the food, but it was quite a while before that food again tasted good to you. In a similar way, bias from past experience can influence what you hear and the meaning you derive from it. If you want to be an effective listener, you must know and admit your biases.

4. *Don't tune out "dry" subjects.* Whenever you are tempted to "tune out" something because you think it will be boring or useless, remember that you cannot evaluate the importance of the message until you have heard it. By

then, it is probably too late to ask the speaker to repeat everything that was said; the opportunity to listen effectively will have passed. As was stated earlier, you must *intend* to listen.

Here are several things you can do to stay focused, even if the subject seems dry.

a. Put yourself in the speaker's place. Try to see the speaker's point of view, and try to understand the speaker's attitude toward the subject.

b. Review frequently what the speaker has said. Try to summarize the message as the speaker would summarize it.

c. Constantly ask yourself positive questions about what the speaker is saying: How can I use this information? How can I share this information with others? What else could be said about this subject?

d. Ask yourself, "What does the speaker know that I don't?"

e. Find at least one major application or conclusion from every message you hear. In other words, ask "what's in this message for me?" Then find the answer.

f. Listen as though you are going to be required to present the same message to a different audience later.

Effective listeners have discovered the value of listening to messages they might have initially considered to be "dry." Sometimes the messages aren't so dry after all. And even when they are, there still may be something of value in them.

5. *Accept responsibility for understanding.* Don't assume this attitude: "Here I am! Teach me—if you can." Such listeners believe knowledge can be poured into them as water is poured into a jug. And they believe the responsibility rests with the one doing the pouring; that is, they believe it is the speaker's fault if effective listening does not occur.

Admittedly, the basic assumption in *Speaking Effectively: A Guide for Air Force Speakers* is that the speaker bears a large responsibility for how well the audience listens. And the speaker's clear organization, engaging support materials, and appropriate delivery do in fact aid listening. But good listeners *are* good because they accept the responsibility for listening and understanding.

6. *Encourage others to talk.* This point applies to those situations in which you find yourself "one-on-one," in a small group discussion, or any other setting that requires exchanges of vocal communication. But you can't listen if no one is talking. The first two guidelines of this section (communicating that you want to listen and being willing to delay judgment) are sources of encouragement to speakers. The discussion below covers several other things you can do.

a. Stop talking. You can't listen if you're talking.

b. Give positive feedback. Look and act interested. Positive head nods, alertness, and smiles—all offer encouragement to the speaker.

c. Ask questions. Questions that show interest and attention encourage both speaker and listener. Show your interest.

d. Empathize with the speaker. Put yourself in the speaker's place; this will help you understand the message.

e. Keep confidences. If the information is sensitive, don't share it with others.

f. Share information. We tend to tell things to those who tell us things. So if you want the speaker to share information with you, share information with the speaker.

What You *Do* about Listening

What we think about listening and what we feel about listening are both fundamental to skillful listening. But the skills themselves are *crucial*. Skills form the psychomotor—the "doing"—element of listening. Here are six crucial skills.

1. *Establish eye contact with the speaker.* Studies show that listening has a positive relationship with eye contact. In other words, the better eye contact you have with the speaker, the better you will listen. And while eye contact is especially important in relationship listening, it is also important for the other kinds of listening: informative, appreciative, critical, discriminative.

There are several things you can do to establish positive eye contact with the speaker:

a. In one-on-one or small group settings, sit or stand where you can look directly at the person doing the speaking.

b. In large groups, sit to the front and center of the audience. You can more easily establish eye contact with the speaker from this vantage point.

c. Don't get so involved in taking notes that you fail to look often at the speaker. The speaker's gestures, movements, and facial expression are often an important part of the message.

d. Resist the temptation to let something about the room, or objects within and around the room, distract you. Focus on the speaker and the message.

e. Don't look at others who enter or leave while the speaker is speaking. This practice not only interrupts your train of thought—it adds to the distraction of the speaker.

f. Speakers sometimes exhibit a visual aid too soon, or neglect to remove it when they have finished using it. Focus on the visual aid only when it is an asset to the point being discussed.

A final point deserves discussion: Never sleep when someone is talking to you! This point may seem self-evident. But let's face it—in the "busyness" of our lives, we tend to become passive whenever we listen. Passivity promotes reduced attention, which in turn allows drowsiness to occur. In most cases, it is better to stand up, or even to leave the room, rather than fall asleep.

2. *Take notes effectively.* Some people recommend that you not take notes so you can focus your attention wholly on what the speaker is saying. This practice works well for listeners who are blessed with a great memory; most of us aren't. Taking notes will not only help you remember, it will help you organize what the speaker is saying. And it may even aid your understanding and retention—after all, effective note taking will require you to think.

There are many different ways to take notes; for example, linear outlining, mindmapping, and key word methodology. Ask different people what method they use, then find what works best for you. Whatever method you select or devise, several things are worth considering.

a. Don't attempt to write everything down. As mentioned earlier, effective listeners focus on the key ideas or main points.

b. Write clearly enough that you can understand your writing later. If not, make certain that you allow time to decipher your notes before they grow "cold." It's disheartening to review your notes two weeks later only to find that they make no sense.

c. Don't rely on listening later to a tape of the speech. Think! Will you have the time? Looking at your notes for five minutes is generally sufficient, and is much more time-efficient than listening to the entire speech again.

d. Circle or highlight the most important points.

3. *Be a physically involved listener.* Just what does this statement mean? As you have already seen, listening requires more than just hearing. You have also seen that making eye contact and taking notes will help to keep you from becoming passive. But there is more: Active listening takes energy and involvement.

Here are some physical behaviors that will ensure your involvement and help your listening.

a. Use good posture. Sit up straight, yet comfortably. Good posture aids breathing and alertness. It also communicates positive interest to the speaker.

b. Follow the speaker. If the speaker moves, turn your head or rotate in your chair to maintain eye contact and attention. This movement also aids in keeping you alert.

c. Don't be a deadpan. Facial expressions, head nods, and tilts of the head show your involvement and provide positive feedback to the speaker.

d. Use your hands not only to take notes, but to show approval by applause when appropriate.

e. Participate when audience involvement is encouraged. Ask questions. Respond when a show of hands is called for. Be an active listener.

f. Smile.

4. *Avoid negative mannerisms.* Everyone has mannerisms. Watch anyone for a period of time and you will be convinced of this fact. If your mannerisms do not cause a negative reaction, don't worry about them. If a mannerism is positive or encouraging and brings a positive response, make a mental note to do it more often. Unfortunately, some mannerisms are negative or distracting. These should be avoided.

Here are some examples of listener mannerisms that either hinder listening or have a negative impact—on the speaker or on other listeners. Avoid these mannerisms.

a. Fidgeting, tapping a pencil, or playing with a rubber band or some other object. The effect on you may be neutral, but such things distract other listeners and are an annoyance to the speaker.

b. Continually looking at the clock or your watch.

c. Reading a paper, balancing a checkbook, rearranging items in your wallet, or engaging in other behavior which takes focus away from the speaker.

d. Displays of arrogance, superiority, or lack of interest in the speaker and message.

In short, any mannerism or behavior that detracts from the speaker or the message should be avoided. Such things hinder the speaker, divert the attention of other listeners, and prevent you from being the best listener you can be.

5. *Exercise your listening muscles.* Actually, there are no muscles technically involved with listening—but this thought reminds us that listening takes practice. Just as an athlete must work out regularly and a musician must practice daily, so you must work consistently to be an effective listener.

But consistent practice in itself is not enough. The difficulty of the message is also important. Exposure to challenging material and difficult listening situations will stretch your ability and build your listening muscles. For example, suppose you knew that you would be required to carry a 50-pound weight one hundred yards in less than a minute. You wouldn't practice by carrying a 30-pound weight. You would practice by carrying at least a 50-pound weight, and you probably would condition yourself to carry it more than 100 yards in less than a minute. With this kind of practice, you would be more than equal to the task. And so it is with listening: Practice to *at least* the level you will be required to perform—perhaps a bit above.

Finally, "s-t-r-e-t-c-h" your vocabulary. We've said this before, but nothing will pay greater listening dividends. Learn the meanings of new words and acronyms. Listen to and read material that contains challenging words. Keep a dictionary nearby. Look up new words as you read them, or jot them down as you listen so you can look up the meanings later.

6. *Follow the Golden Rule.* Do unto others as you would have them do unto you. The central focus of all effective communication is "other directedness." There are exceptions to most other listening rules. For example, there are times when a listener shouldn't prepare; preparation may prevent openness to new ideas. There are times when the objective is not to focus on key points, but to listen for subordinate ideas or supporting material. There are times

when we should not delay judgment—we must act! But while these and other rules have exceptions, not so for the Golden Rule. The effective listener is *always* other directed, focused on the other person.

Be the kind of listener you want others to be when you are talking. Ask "How would I want others to listen to me?" That's how to be an effective listener.